HAWAII FOOD GUIDE

UNIQUE FOODS FROM HAWAII YOU'VE GOT TO TRY

ETHAN FROST

Copyright © 2016

WHY YOU SHOULD READ THIS BOOK

This book will help you get a good picture of some of the most loved and popular foods of Hawaii. Hawaii is a unique place with so many ethnicities and cultures. The amazing thing you may notice is that Hawaiian food and the culture of the island go hand in hand. I hope that you will be able to experience all of the foods in this book sometime in your life. Or at least many of them on your next vacation to the islands. Or if possible, maybe you can even find a way to get a hold of them or try to make some of them where you are at right now!

TABLE OF CONTENTS

CHAPTER 1. BACKGROUND OF HAWAIIAN ISLAND FOOD

Hawaii's food and culture are very very intertwined and connected. It is a melting pot of local and imported foods. One of the blessings of Hawaii is being able to try many different types of food. Food is pretty much a way of life in Hawaii, but its roots can be traced back to the timeline of Hawaii's history. Many centuries ago the Polynesians settled in Hawaii, lived off the land and food they had brought from other areas of Polynesia in their natural environment. Foods such as fish, taro, and coconuts were a big part of their way of being sustained.

As time went on pineapple and sugarcane plantations in Hawaii needed workers. People from many different places such as China, Japan, Portugal, and the Philippines came to work as laborers. The effect of this was many new ethnic foods blending into the Hawaii cultural landscape. These foods were shared between the many different peoples, and amazingly seem to work together to have what we now have today. In Hawaii, although there are many different kinds of people it is a very relaxed atmosphere. People are laid back and get along well even between ethnicities.

Today if you enter any supermarket or grocery store in the islands you will have many foods that are exactly similar to the U.S. mainland. The people of Hawaii in many places (especially Oahu) are very modern and enjoy things that every other American for the most part enjoys. The difference is that about at least a third of most grocery stores in Hawaii really show the uniqueness of Hawaii's food culture. You will find many ingredients, fresh food, and manufactured food that is very different than most places in America. Macadamia nuts, poke, poi, are some of the foods you will be able to get at just about any grocery store. So Hawaii continues to be a place of great Aloha (love), weather, as well as food! The restaurants and eateries also reflect the food of Hawaii. It's not unlikely to have an authentic Chinese, Filipino, Hawaiian, and Vietnamese restaurant side by side in one shopping area. In this book, I have highlighted many of the most well known and enjoyed foods that are unique to Hawaii.

CHAPTER 2. TYPES OF FOOD ENJOYED IN HAWAII

NATIVE HAWAIIAN FOOD

The ancient Hawaiians were very healthy people who lived off the land. They had their own way of life and their own diet. They had their own set of diverse foods. Some of their diet consisted of foods brought by Polynesians settlers in Hawaii, as well as some foods that were indigenous to Hawaii. Although there weren't that many! These foods came before the Japanese, Europeans, and Filipinos, etc. came in contact with the native Hawaiian people and Hawaiian islands. Taro, Ulu, Coconuts, and Kava are a few of the staples eaten those early days. These foods were both healthy and nutritious. In the early days, meat was not as popular and was eaten sparingly. Interestingly there was a Hawaiian set of rules in ancient Hawaii called "Kapu" long ago. One of the Kapu laws was that women and men could not eat together, and some foods weren't freely enjoyed by both sexes under Kapu. Kapu was abolished in 1819 when powerful Hawaiian queens chose to have it ended. Free eating, as well as many other foreign values, continued to grow in the islands at that time. Fishing was popular with the early Hawaiians as well as other seafood. One very popular food to native Hawaii is Poi. It is made from the stem or corm of a vegetable plant called a Kalo (Taro). It is smashed continually till it becomes a wet consistency. Hawaiians are the only people known to make Poi and it was a very popular and sacred food in their culture. Native Hawaiian foods are now still in the culture of Hawaii. They have mixed in well and have been adapted to this current time. Although they aren't as common and eaten as frequently as long ago, a few authentic Hawaiian type restaurants have continued to serve these foods daily.

WESTERN INFLUENCE

Over the years many Europeans, starting back to the colonial days introduced new foods to Hawaii. Today in Hawaii McDonald's, Burger King, and Chili's are popular. Any food that is part of a normal diet in the USA is found and eaten in Hawaii for the most part. Over the last 200 years, many Caucasians have been influential in the cultivation and exportation of many popular foods such as pineapple and sugarcane.

Japanese Food in Hawaii

There may be more Japanese restaurants in Hawaii than just about any other ethnic food. Japanese laborers came in the 1800's and brought along many of their foods as well. These laborers came and adapted to the conditions of Hawaii and became "locals" as well, blending into the Hawaiian population. Over the years many Japanese stores and business continue to thrive on the islands. The Japanese makeup about 17% of Hawaii's population. Sushi which is a popular Japanese dish, is very very popular in Hawaii. Quite a few other Japanese foods have become part of the Hawaii food landscape.

Chinese Food in Hawaii

Like the Japanese, Chinese laborers were part of the growth of Hawaii and it's history. Today you can find many Chinese restaurants that are similar to the ones you will find anywhere else. These restaurants are popular in Hawaii and the locals are pretty much adept at ordering and dining at any Chinese restaurant. Along with that, many Chinese foods mixed in well and became fused with other foods in Hawaii. So quite a few Chinese foods are now commonly eaten by everyone in Hawaii.

Other Important Ethnic Food Cultures

Other important food cultures in Hawaii are Filipino, Portuguese, Vietnamese, Korean, as well as some others. Adobo and Lumpia have become popular dishes in Hawaii. Kim Chee which is seasoned vegetables is a well-known

Korean dish with locals as well. Another dish brought by the Vietnamese is Pho.

SPAM IN HAWAII

One question that has been asked is "why does Hawaii love Spam so much?". As a person who has spent a lot of time in Hawaii, my answer would be the same as many other locals. That answer would be, "I don't know, we just do". Hawaii is such a melting pot that sometimes it's hard to find a starting point or reason. To many in Hawaii, things are just the way they are. The locals of Hawaii know what they like, but aren't really that big on the reasons why or getting into long discussions. It's just a local attitude where it's better to be laid back and relax than to think too hard about it! Although that is true, I will go into some of the interesting facts about Spam in Hawaii.

Spam was first introduced in 1937 and became popular during WWII. It is precooked meat in a can. Hawaii eats more Spam than any other area of the world. During WWII Spam became very important for feeding soldiers. Since Hawaii played a major part in WWII, you can see the connection there. Spam also mixed well over the years with the many different cultures of Hawaii, in terms of food. Spam goes great with rice of course, and many cultures in Hawaii have rice as a major staple. In Hawaii, Spam is not seen as a poor man's type food. Although it may be seen that way in other places, that stigma is never seen in Hawaii. In Hawaii, there are many recipes for Spam. When mixed with a lot of the flavors and spices that are available on the islands it tastes great!

Chapter 3. Hawaii's Unique Foods

In this chapter are 17 of the most loved foods today in Hawaii. Some of them are totally unique to Hawaii and are not really eaten anywhere else in the world. Some of the others you will read about here grew to be loved over time as the people of different cultures that lived in Hawaii shared their food amongst each other on the island through the years. The other foods here may be available or could be made just about anywhere in the USA, but have become very popular in Hawaii.

Poke

"Poke" in Hawaiian means slice or cut. Poke is an appetizer that is made of usually raw fish, octopus or Aku, but many other variations exist. Poke seasonings in Hawaii include green onions, soy sauce, and sesame oil. It may be Hawaii's favorite food and is healthy and delicious. It even has picked up some popularity on the U.S. mainland. It is available at just about every grocery market in Hawaii as well.

SPAM MUSUBI

Spam Musubi is a very popular snack that is a daily staple for locals in Hawaii. Musubis can be found just about everywhere on the islands. The people of Hawaii definitely have a great love for Spam, and probably eat more Spam than any other place/people in the world. It all started around world war II and due to the influence of Hawaii's local Japanese population, the popularity of these musubis grew. A Spam musubi consists of one cooked slice of Spam on top of a block of white rice. The Spam and rice are then wrapped in a strip of nori dried seaweed. There are other variations as well such as an addition of egg or teriyaki flavored spam musubi.

MANAPUA

This is a food that is a round white bun often filled with pork filling. It is usually steamed or baked. It can be filled with different flavored filling such as curry chicken, sweet bean, vegetables, char siu. Some manapua specialty stores have even begun selling pizza, ham and cheese, and turkey melt flavors! It is also often readily available in Hawaii at convenience stores, as well as the frozen section of most grocery stores. Chinese immigrants brought their culture and food to the Hawaiian islands back in the 19th century. Food vendors hit the streets with these manapua snacks which led to it being ingrained in Hawaii culture. Char Siu Bao was the original name of the Manapua. Prices range from about $1-2 dollars.

LOCO MOCO

The Loco Moco is a very popular food enjoyed by people in Hawaii daily and year around. It is white rice, a hamburger patty, fried egg, and gravy. It began being served in a restaurant in Hawaii a few decades ago and was inexpensive to make. It is now on the menu at many restaurants in Hawaii that serve local food, and even in Hawaiian themed restaurants on the U.S. mainland. It was once highlighted on the Food Network by celebrity chef Guy Fieri.

PLATE LUNCH

Popular "plate lunches" in Hawaii are chicken katsu, teri beef, kalua pork, lemon chicken, and hamburger steak. In totality, it will consist of a meal on a paper plate with rice, macaroni salad, and the entree. The origin and beginnings of plate lunches in Hawaii are still debated, but there is no doubt it has grown into a big part of Hawaii's food culture. Two of the most famous places to go for a plate lunch in Hawaii is L&L Drive Inn and Rainbow Drive Inn.

Saimin

Saimin is a favorite fast food in the islands. It is a soup and noodle meal that began in China and continued on by immigrant nationalities in Hawaii. It was developed during Hawaii's plantation days. It can be found at most local restaurants and even at Hawaii McDonald's locations. There are also many saimin specialty shops that serve premium saimin as well. It is pretty much a comfort food on the islands.

ARARE

These Japanese rice crackers called "arare" or "kaki mochi" are a favorite snack for locals. You can find them in just about every grocery store on the islands. They are the Japanese equivalent to what potato chips are in the US. These were brought by Japanese plantation workers in the early to mid 1800's. This crunchy crackers are made of glutinous rice and flavored with soy sauce. They do come in different size and shapes, some are even covered with dry seaweed. They are low in fat but high in sodium.

Macadamia Nuts

These are the most sought after nuts in Hawaii. In 1881 The first macadamia nut tree was planted in Hawaii. It amazingly grew very well. Over the years they have been cultivated well on the islands and have grown into a major multimillion dollar business. Today macadamia nuts are readily available everywhere and are most popular with tourists. Chocolate covered macadamias are a well-known treat. Many new flavors of macadamia are being sold now such as Maui onion. Mauna Loa is the most famous brand.

MOCHI

A traditionally Japanese food mochi is made of glutinous rice. It is made by pounding the steamed glutinous rice. Many restaurants and local stores specialize in this snack and have different flavors. It is sweet and soft kind of like candy. There is a vast array that you can sample and try, such as azuki, sweet potato or even peanut butter flavor. The flavors that are available seem to be endless.

PINEAPPLE

Hawaii is very famous for the production of pineapple. Pineapple is not exclusive just to Hawaii, but companies such as Dole Pineapple have become known worldwide. In 1922 James Dole began the largest pineapple plantation in the world. He produced over 75% of the world's pineapple. Hawaii today continues to supply many pineapple products to the world. It is a favorite of those coming to Hawaii for vacation. Many tourists enjoy taking whole pineapples home with them from vacation.

SHAVE ICE

Shave ice is an iconic must have treat for those who live and visit the Hawaiian islands. It is a highly regarded "must have" at least once on any Hawaii vacation. Shave ice has been available on the islands for decades and is basically a syrup flavored snow cone. At times ice cream can be added as well. Two of the most popular spots to eat shave ice in Hawaii are Matsumoto and Waiola Shave ice. Many of these shops have been coming up with new exotic flavors.

Poi

Poi is made from pounded Hawaiian Taro root, known in Hawaii as "Kalo". It is a sticky starchy food. It can be doughy or even have a liquid consistency. When it is fresh it is sweet. As time passes it becomes sour. It has been a staple of the native Hawaiian diet for centuries.

GARLIC SHRIMP

Many tourists and locals have experienced a meal from a
"garlic shrimp truck" in Hawaii. These trucks throughout
Hawaii serve garlic shrimp that is simply delicious.
Hopefully, many people that are not in Hawaii will get a
chance to experience this. An interesting thing is that many
people have found Hawaiian Garlic Shrimp recipes online
and have tried it at home!

WHITE RICE

White rice has been popular in the islands since Chinese
immigrant workers arrived. At first it had to be imported, but
because of its popularity, it began to be grown in Hawaii.
Some rice started to be grown in the islands. Eventually

Mainland rice became more popular and it was shipped into Hawaii, in large quantities. Today rice is a main fixture of local culture. Almost every family seems to eat rice daily. It is the most important staple for Hawaii people.

MALASADAS

A Malasada is a portuguese donut with a hole and is a local icon. They are yeast leaven donuts enriched with eggs, butter, and sometimes evaporated of fresh milk. They are then fried and rolled in sugar. They are often unfilled but can be filled with fillings such as custard. Many immigrant workers found their way to Hawaii back in the 19th century. Malasadas were brought by the Azores. The most popular malasadas in Hawaii are made by Hawaii's Leonard's Bakery.

LAU LAU

Lau Lau is a native Hawaii dish. It is a taro and ti leaf filled with usually pork as well as a piece of salt cod (butterfish). There are quite a few variations that can be made with it as well. Other Polynesian cultures have something similar to Lau Lau interestingly. It can be found as many restaurants, even well-known ones in Hawaii.

SPAM OR PORTUGUESE SAUSAGE, EGGS, AND RICE

This is a breakfast meal that is very easy to make. This is one case where the whole seems to be much better than the parts! Sometimes Spam is substituted for Portuguese sausage. This meal is offered at quite a few restaurants. The cool thing is in Hawaii even national chain Mcdonald's has added it to the breakfast menu. This is very popular with the locals, and many of them shop for ingredients at the grocery store to cook at home at least once a week.

Ulu

Ulu was one of the plants that the Polynesians brought with them when they first settled in Hawaii. There are many ways it can be prepared. The Ulu tree and breadfruit have many uses as well. The tree could produce cloth and canoes.

CONCLUSION

Thank you for reading this book I hope you were able to get a good feels for some of the most popular and enjoyed foods Hawaii has to offer. The thing is that these foods became very popular in Hawaii for a reason. It seems that with all that has happened in Hawaii history these foods seemed to organically turn out to be the most loved of all time. This mix of the people, families, and foods they enjoy continues to this day. Although there are some more foods that could be added to the list. I'm sure some natives of Hawaii would love to add some more in, but maybe we'll have a second edition of this book with more foods!

That's great, because there are so many foods to love in Hawaii the sampling and enjoyment of them can continue to be loved, discussed, enjoyed, and debated.

One last thing!

If you received value from this book, I ask that you please consider posting a review at the end of this book.

Thanks again!

Other Hawaii Books Available by Ethan Frost on Kindle:

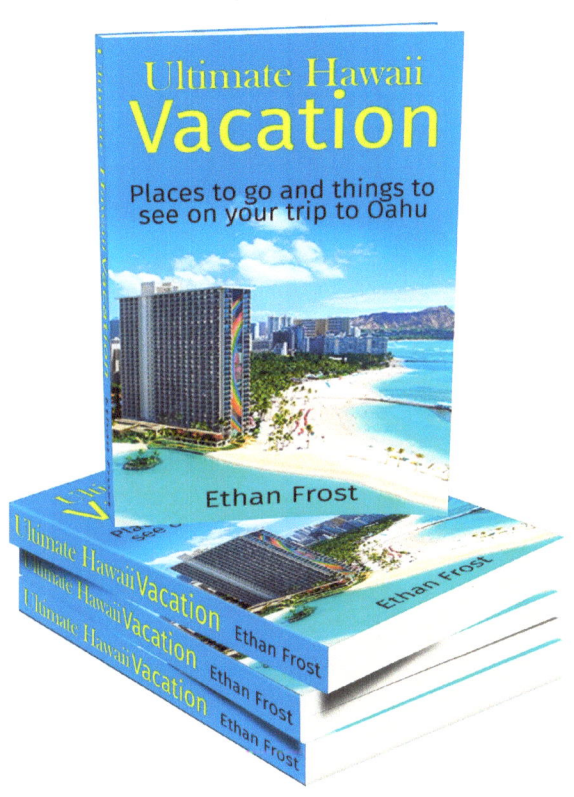

www.ingramcontent.com/pod-product-compliance
Lightning Source LLC
Chambersburg PA
CBHW040820200526

45159CB00024B/3073